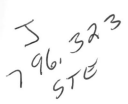

The Illinois Fighting Illini™

Fighting Illini®

BY
MARK STEWART

Content Consultant
Matt Zeysing
Historian and Archivist
The Naismith Memorial Basketball Hall of Fame

NORWOOD HOUSE 🏠 PRESS
CHICAGO, ILLINOIS

Norwood House Press
P.O. Box 316598
Chicago, Illinois 60631

For information regarding Norwood House Press, please visit our website at:
www.norwoodhousepress.com or call 866-565-2900.

All photos courtesy of Getty Images except the following:
University of Illinois (6, 17, 36 left), A.S. Barnes & Co. (7),
Associated Press (10, 18, 19, 24, 26, 29, 31, 33, 34, 39 bottom, 41 bottom left),
Author's Collection (14, 37 top left, 40, 41 bottom right), Elbak Publishing Company (22),
Icon SMI (15, 21, 25), Washington Bullets (36 right), TCMA, Ltd. (39),
Time Inc./Sports Illustrated (40 top right), Matt Richman (48).
Cover Photo: Jonathan Daniel/Getty Images

Special thanks to Topps, Inc.

Editor: Mike Kennedy
Designer: Ron Jaffe
Project Management: Black Book Partners, LLC.
Editorial Production: Jessica McCulloch
Research: Joshua Zaffos
Special thanks to Bobby Hall

Library of Congress Cataloging-in-Publication Data

Stewart, Mark, 1960-
   The Illinois fighting Illini / by Mark Stewart.
      p. cm.
   Includes bibliographical references and index.
   Summary: "Presents the history and accomplishments of the University of
Illinois Fighting Illini basketball team. Includes highlights of players,
coaches, and awards, longstanding rivalries, quotes, timeline, maps,
glossary, and websites"--Provided by publisher.
   ISBN-13: 978-1-59953-365-0 (library edition : alk. paper)
   ISBN-10: 1-59953-365-0 (library edition : alk. paper)
   1. University of Illinois at Urbana-Champaign--Basketball--History--
Juvenile literature. 2. Fighting Illini (Basketball team)--History--Juvenile
literature. I. Title.
   GV885.43.U5S84 2010
   796.323'6309773--dc22
                                                    2009033811

Manufactured in the United States of America in North Mankato, Minnesota.
N144—012010

COVER PHOTO: Illinois fans cheer on their team during a 2005–06 game.

Table of Contents

SPORTS WORDS & VOCABULARY WORDS: In this book, you will find many words that are new to you. You may also see familiar words used in new ways. The glossary on page 46 gives the meanings of basketball words, as well as "everyday" words that have special basketball meanings. These words appear in **bold type** throughout the book. The glossary on page 47 gives the meanings of vocabulary words that are not related to basketball. They appear in ***bold italic type*** throughout the book.

Meet the Fighting Illini

Basketball is a way of life in Illinois. From the farm towns to the *suburbs* to the cities, young players dream big and shoot for the stars. Many grow up hoping to take the court for the University of Illinois. The *campus* is in the town of Champaign. The school is the oldest and largest of the state's many fine universities.

In 1982, the school's name was officially changed to the University of Illinois–Urbana-Champaign. But when you say "Illinois basketball," fans know what you're talking about. The same is true when you say the team's nickname, the Fighting Illini.

This book tells the story of the Illini. Their great stars sometimes seem as if they stepped out of a Hollywood movie. Their fantastic finishes sound like make-believe tales. The fact is that the Illinois basketball story is very real and very true. And it's one of the best you'll ever hear.

The Illini talk over their game plan during the 2004–05 season.

Way Back When

Basketball was a popular sport at Illinois in the beginning of the 20th *century*. The school actually had a women's team long before the men's team started in 1905. The sport really took off on campus after Ralph Jones arrived. He taught his players an exciting new style of play with lots of running and passing. Some say this was basketball's first **fast break** offense.

The Illini had several good players in their early years, including Ray Woods and Chuck Carney. Each was hailed as the top player in the nation. Woods led the team to a perfect 16–0 record in 1914–15. Carney was an **All-American** in football and basketball in the 1920s. He set a **Big Ten Conference** scoring record that lasted for nearly two *decades*.

Doug Mills became the team's coach in the 1930s. He led the Illini to the Big Ten championship in his first year. In the early 1940s, Mills put together one of the game's most famous teams. Everyone knew the squad as the "Whiz Kids." Their stars were Andy Phillip and Gene Vance. They pushed the ball up the court again and again and again—until their opponents were gasping for air.

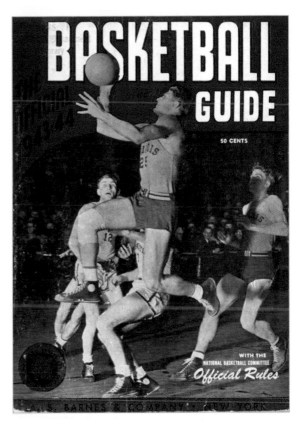

The Whiz Kids were expected to win the 1943 championship of the **National Collegiate Athletic Association (NCAA),** but the players had other ideas. World War II had begun, and the United States military needed all the help it could get. The team's starting five—Phillip, Vance, Jack Smiley, Ken Menke, and Art Mathisen—skipped the **NCAA Tournament** so they could all go into military service together. They became true "national champions" without ever making a single basket. All but Mathisen returned for one fabulous season after the war. They led Illinois to a second-place finish in the Big Ten in 1946–47.

The Illini continued to put great teams on the floor. They won three Big Ten titles and went to the **Final Four** three times from 1949 to 1952. Harry Combes was the coach of those teams. His star players were Dike Eddleman, Don Sunderlage, and Johnny Kerr.

LEFT: Doug Mills, the coach who led the famous "Whiz Kids" team.
ABOVE: A 1943 basketball guide shows Gene Vance on the cover.

After four decades of winning basketball, the Illini began to struggle. From the mid-1950s until the 1980s, they won the Big Ten championship just one time. Illinois still had some excellent players during this period, including Don Ohl, Mannie Jackson, Govoner Vaughn, Dave Downey, Skip Thoren, Donnie Freeman, Rich Jones, Jim Dawson, Dave Scholz, Mike Price, Nick Weatherspoon, Mark Smith, and Eddie Johnson.

The man who rebuilt Illinois into a powerhouse was Lou Henson. He coached the team for 21 years and guided the Illini to the NCAA Tournament 12 times. Facing Illinois during the 1980s was no fun. Stars during this era included Derek Harper, Ken Norman, and Bruce Douglas. The 1988–89 squad was especially talented. Kenny Battle, Kendall Gill, Nick Anderson, Steve Bardo, and Marcus Liberty led a high-scoring group nicknamed the "Flyin' Illini." That season, they soared to the top spot in the national rankings.

After 423 victories Henson stepped down, and Lon Kruger took over. In 1997–98, Kruger won the Big Ten championship with five seniors in the starting **lineup**, including captains Jerry Hester, Brian Johnson, and Matt Heldman. Kruger coached four seasons at the end of the 1990s before taking a job in the **National Basketball Association (NBA)**. The Illini were ranked in the Top 25 three times. More important, they created a foundation for the great teams to come.

Jerry Hester floats to the basket for a layup.

21st Century

The success of the Illinois basketball team at the end of the 1990s carried right into the 21st century. Bill Self was hired to coach the team, and he won the Big Ten title in each of his first two seasons. It had been 90 years since a coach had done that! Self's teams starred Cory Bradford, Brian Cook, and Frank Williams. The 2000–01 squad finished the year ranked fourth in the nation.

In 2003, Bruce Weber took over as coach. He *inherited* an amazing **roster** that included Dee Brown, Deron Williams, Roger Powell, Luther Head, and James Augustine. In 2004–05, the Illini tied an NCAA record with 37 victories and made it all the way to the national championship game.

Illinois won because of its hardworking and unselfish lineup. Year after year, players who could have been superstars on lesser teams chose to wear the orange and navy blue of the Illini. They played good **team basketball** and found new and exciting ways to win. These players achieved a new standard for success and set an example for all the Illinois teams that followed.

James Augustine and Dee Brown share a laugh during a 2005–06 game.

Home Court

The Illini have played their home games in Assembly Hall since the early 1960s. Although the arena is old, it still has a modern look and feel. It was designed by an *architect* named Max Abramovitz, who was one of the school's most famous graduates.

Assembly Hall has an unusual dome, which is supported by steel wire straps. It is bright white and glows in the nighttime sky. The arena is the second largest in the state after the United Center, where the Chicago Bulls of the NBA play their home games.

Assembly Hall got its name because it was built for—what else?—assemblies. The university needed a building that could seat thousands of students. By the 1960s, as the school continued to grow, its old auditorium was just too small. Assembly Hall was built, and the Illini still use it today.

BY THE NUMBERS

- *There are 16,618 seats for basketball in Assembly Hall.*
- *The arena cost $8 million to build in 1963.*
- *The dome is supported by more than 600 miles of quarter-inch steel straps.*
- *The building is 400 feet from side to side and 128 feet tall.*

Assembly Hall is a sea of orange when Illinois plays.

Dressed for Success

The Illinois athletic teams have been known as the Fighting Illini since the 1920s. *Illini* is another name for people who live in Illinois. The name was first used to honor soldiers from the state who fought in World War I. Later in the 1920s, the school added a **mascot**. He was called "Chief Illiniwek" to recognize Sioux tribes. For many decades, the Illinois **logo** was a picture of an Indian chief with a big headdress.

In recent years, Native American groups have objected to these types of **symbols**. In 2007, Illinois agreed to "retire" Chief Illiniwek during a basketball game. He received a standing **ovation** from the students as a farewell.

For most of the 1800s, the official school colors changed often. The sports teams switched permanently to orange and navy blue in 1894. Today, the team's logo is an *I* with the "new" school colors.

Andy Phillip models the Illinois uniform from the 1940s.

UNIFORM BASICS

The basketball uniform is very simple. It consists of a roomy top and baggy shorts.

- The top hangs from the shoulders, with big "scoops" for the arms and neck. This style has not changed much over the years.

- Shorts, however, have changed a lot. They used to be very short, so players could move their legs freely. In the last 20 years, shorts have gotten longer and much baggier.

Basketball uniforms look the same as they did long ago ... until you look very closely. In the old days, the shorts had belts and buckles. The tops were made of a thick cotton called "jersey," which got very heavy when players sweated. Later, uniforms were made of shiny *satin*. They may have looked great, but they did not "breathe." As a result, players got very hot! Today, most uniforms are made of *synthetic* materials that soak up sweat and keep the body cool.

Chester Frazier dribbles the ball wearing the team's 2008–09 home uniform.

We're Number 1!

In the early years of basketball, there were no national tournaments, no college champions, and no **Most Valuable Player (MVP)** or Player of the Year trophies. In the 1930s, the Helms Athletic Foundation decided to go "back in time" and name the top players and teams from each season. Sometimes this caused big arguments.

When the experts got to the 1914–15 season, however, there was no debate at all. Illinois was the nation's best team, and Ray Woods was the top player. Coach Ralph Jones was in his third year with the Illini that season. His team passed the ball so quickly that many opponents simply could not keep up. No one could stop the Illini offense.

Woods was an amazing athlete. He outjumped opponents for rebounds, outfought them for **loose balls**, and rarely let his man score. When Illinois had the ball, Woods would bark out plays and then deliver perfect passes to his teammates. In the season's biggest game, he made the winning shot. The Illini finished with a perfect 16–0 record.

Nearly three decades later, Illinois was once again on top of the college basketball world. In 1942–43, the team known as the Whiz Kids stormed through its schedule, finishing with a 17–1 record. Their

The 1942–43 team watches coach Doug Mills sketch out a play.

greatest victory came in February against Wisconsin. A year earlier, the Illini had made headlines by defeating the Badgers, who were the national champions at the time. Now Illinois had a chance to prove itself again.

The Illini relied on the starting five of Gene Vance, Andy Phillip, Art Mathisen, Jack Smiley, and Ken Menke. They were sensational in their rematch with the Badgers. Phillip and Mathisen scored at will. Vance and Menke controlled the backboards. Smiley held Wisconsin star John Kotz to zero points. Illinois won in a blowout, 50–26. There was no question which team was the nation's best.

Unfortunately, the Illini would not get to display their talent in the NCAA Tournament. With World War II underway, Mathisen, Menke, and Smiley were drafted into the military. Vance and Phillip could have stayed and played, but they decided to enlist and join their teammates. They would let other teams fight over the national championship.

It took more than 60 years for Illinois to reach #1 again. The team celebrated its 100th season in 2004–05 by winning its first 29 games in a row. After defeating top-ranked Wake Forest in early December, the Illini were the nation's best team for the rest of the regular season. The starting five of Deron Williams, Dee Brown, James Augustine, Luther Head, and Roger Powell worked together like a finely tuned engine.

The Illini finished first in the conference, and then won the **Big Ten Tournament**. In the NCAA Tournament, they won their first three games easily. Against Arizona, they scored a thrilling overtime victory to move into the Final Four. The team's magical run lasted until the championship game. They were beaten by the North Carolina Tar Heels. Although Illinois finished second for the season, they had won 37 games. No team in college basketball history had ever achieved a higher total.

LEFT: James Augustine and Luther Head bottle up Chris Paul during the Illini's victory over Wake Forest.   **ABOVE**: Roger Powell leads the celebration after the team's win over Louisville in the 2005 Final Four.

Go-To Guys

GENE VANCE   6′ 3″ Guard

• BORN: 2/25/1923   • PLAYED FOR VARSITY: 1941–42 TO 1942–43 & 1946–47

Gene Vance was a swift, strong guard who attacked enemy defenses. He was named First-Team **All-Big Ten** in his first two seasons. He returned to Illinois after World War II and played his senior season. Later, Vance became the school's ***athletic director***.

NICK WEATHERSPOON   6′ 7″ Forward

• BORN: 7/20/1950   • DIED: 10/17/2008   • PLAYED FOR VARSITY: 1970–71 TO 1972–73

If opponents didn't **double-team** Nick Weatherspoon, he was nearly unstoppable. "Spoon" set school records by averaging 20.9 points and 11.4 rebounds per game for his career. He was a First-Team All-American in 1972–73.

DEREK HARPER   6′ 4″ Guard

• BORN: 10/13/1961   • PLAYED FOR VARSITY: 1980–81 TO 1982–83

Whenever the Illini needed a big play, they looked to Derek Harper. His basket at the end of the 1982–83 season sent Illinois to the NCAA Tournament. Harper was First Team All-Big Ten that year. He later became a first-round **draft pick** of the Dallas Mavericks.

FRANK WILLIAMS   6′ 3″ Guard

- BORN: 2/25/1980
- PLAYED FOR VARSITY: 1999–00 TO 2001–02

Frank Williams was a First Team All-American and the Big Ten Player of the Year in 2000–01. Thanks to his great shooting, passing, and defense, Illinois reached the top of the conference two years in a row.

DERON WILLIAMS   6′ 3″ Guard

- BORN: 6/26/1984
- PLAYED FOR VARSITY: 2002–03 TO 2004–05

Deron Williams was a tough, physical player who led the Illini to the NCAA championship game in 2005. His clutch **3-pointers** against Arizona sparked an amazing *comeback* that put Illinois in the Final Four. That season, Williams was named to the **All-Final Four** team and honored as First Team All-Big Ten.

Frank Williams

DEE BROWN   6′ 0″ Guard

- BORN: 8/17/1984   • PLAYED FOR VARSITY: 2002–03 TO 2005–06

When **playmaker** Dee Brown walked onto the court with his bright orange headband, the Illini and their fans believed they couldn't lose. He teamed with Deron Williams and Luther Head to give Illinois a great backcourt. In 2004–05, Brown was named an All-American and Player of the Year by *The Sporting News*.

ANDY PHILLIP   6′ 2″ Guard/Forward

- Born: 3/7/1922   • Died: 4/29/2001
- Played for Varsity: 1941–42 to 1942–43 & 1946–47

Andy Phillip set a conference scoring record as a sophomore and then broke it as a junior. He was the ultimate team player, filling in at several positions and playing hard at both ends of the court. Phillip was a First Team All-American three times—as much for his quick hands and great passing as his shooting touch.

JOHNNY KERR   6′ 9″ Center

- Born: 7/17/1932   • Died: 2/26/2009
- Played for Varsity: 1951–52 to 1953–54

Johnny "Red" Kerr led the Illini to the Final Four in his first season and was the Big Ten's MVP as a senior. Kerr averaged more than 25 points a game in 1953–54 and graduated as the school's all-time leading scorer.

DONNIE FREEMAN   6′ 3″ Guard

- Born: 7/18/1944
- Played for Varsity: 1963–64 to 1966–67

When fast-moving, smooth-shooting Donnie Freeman set his sights on the basket, he was almost impossible to stop. Freeman averaged 27.8 points per game as a senior and was a First Team All-American.

KENDALL GILL   6′ 5″ Guard

- BORN: 5/25/1968
- PLAYED FOR VARSITY: 1986–87 TO 1989–90

Kendall Gill was an excellent **all-around** player who led the Big Ten in scoring as a senior. He was an equally talented defender, too. The Illini reached the NCAA Tournament in each of Gill's four seasons.

NICK ANDERSON   6′ 6″ Forward

- BORN: 1/20/1968
- PLAYED FOR VARSITY: 1987–88 TO 1988–89

Nick Anderson shot the ball with confidence whether he was **driving** to the basket for a dunk or launching a 3-pointer. In 1989, he made an amazing 30-foot shot to beat the powerhouse Indiana Hoosiers on their home court. Later that year, Anderson led the team to the Final Four.

DEON THOMAS   6′ 9″ Forward

- BORN: 2/24/1971   • PLAYED FOR VARSITY: 1990–91 TO 1993–94

When Deon Thomas had the basketball, it usually took two players to stop him. By the time he was done at Illinois, he was the school's top all-time scorer and the second-best rebounder. Thomas also set a new mark with 177 blocked shots.

LEFT: As this photo shows, Johnny Kerr was also good at keeping the other team from scoring.   **ABOVE**: Nick Anderson

DIKE EDDLEMAN   6′ 3″ Forward

• BORN: 12/27/1922   • DIED: 8/1/2001   • PLAYED FOR VARSITY: 1946–47 TO 1948–49

During the 1940s, the eyes of young sports fans everywhere lit up when they heard the name Dike Eddleman. Besides leading Illinois to the Final Four, he also starred in the **Rose Bowl** for the school's football team. In 1948, Eddleman won a silver medal at the **Olympics** in the high jump.

EDDIE JOHNSON   6′ 7″ Forward

• BORN: 5/1/1959   • PLAYED FOR VARSITY: 1977–78 TO 1980–81

Illinois hadn't made a **postseason** appearance for 15 years when Eddie Johnson joined the team. By the time his career was done, he held the school scoring record and had led the Illini back to the NCAA Tournament. Johnson's great shooting earned him the nickname "Mr. Automatic."

BRUCE DOUGLAS   6′ 3″ Guard

• BORN: 4/9/1964

• PLAYED FOR VARSITY: 1982–83 TO 1985–86

Games often are decided by a great pass or a perfectly timed defensive play. Both were specialties of Bruce Douglas during his career. He led the Illini to the NCAA Tournament four times and graduated as the Big Ten's all-time leader in steals and **assists**.

KENNY BATTLE   6′ 6″ Forward

- BORN: 10/10/1964
- PLAYED FOR VARSITY: 1987–88 TO 1988–89

Was anyone more fun to watch than Kenny Battle? Not if you loved a great dunk. Battle was a leader on the great Illinois teams of the late 1980s. No one could bring a crowd to its feet like he could.

BRIAN COOK   6′ 9″ Forward

- BORN: 12/4/1980
- PLAYED FOR VARSITY: 1999–00 TO 2002–03

Whenever a ball clanked off the rim, it wasn't long before Brian Cook wrapped his hands around it. Cook was the Illini's "man in the middle" for four seasons. He was the Big Ten scoring champ and Player of the Year as a senior.

JAMES AUGUSTINE   6′ 10″ Forward/Center

- BORN: 2/27/1984   • PLAYED FOR VARSITY: 2002–03 TO 2005 06

James Augustine's strong play near the basket gave teammates like Luther Head and Dee Brown more room to work on the edge of the offense. He was the first player in school history with 1,000 points and 1,000 rebounds. Augustine was named the **Most Outstanding Player (MOP)** in the 2005 Big Ten Tournament.

LEFT: Bruce Douglas
ABOVE: Brian Cook

On the Sidelines

Illinois has a great coaching *tradition*. Ralph Jones and J. Craig Ruby were excellent teachers and motivators. They helped the Illini rise to the top of the Big Ten four times from 1915 to 1935. Doug Mills and Harry Combes coached the team during its most successful seasons. Mills had been a star athlete at Illinois in the 1920s. He was famous for leading the Whiz Kids, but he did a great job after those players left for World War II. Mills handed the coaching job to Combes in 1947. He had played for Mills in the 1930s. Combes taught his players to win games with defense.

The Illini's most famous coach was Lou Henson. He led the team for two decades starting in the mid-1970s. Henson studied the game carefully and made sure his players were always prepared, especially on defense. He took Illinois to the Final Four in 1989, but his best season may have been 1983–84. That year, the Illini lost five games by a total of only 16 points.

After Henson left Illinois, Lon Kruger, Bill Self, and Bruce Weber all led the team to conference titles. Kruger and Self were smart, friendly coaches who were admired greatly. Weber was hardworking, serious, and an excellent leader.

Lou Henson cuts down the net after a big victory during the 1988–89 season.

Rivals

In the Big Ten, every game is a big game. However, the biggest *rival* of the Illini does not play in the conference. The Missouri Tigers are part of a different conference. The school is located less than 300 miles to the west of Champaign, in the town of Columbia. Illinois often competes against Missouri to **recruit** the same high school stars. Many of the players on the Illini and Tigers played with or against each other when they were younger.

The annual Illinois–Missouri game is usually held in December. Fans call it the "Braggin' Rights" game because the winning team gets to brag about its victory for a year. The game is played in St. Louis, Missouri, which is less than three hours from each campus. The winner gets to keep the Braggin' Rights trophy on its side of a special showcase. On the other side is a sign that reads, "The Trophy Belongs Here Next Year."

Missouri fans say that the greatest moment in this rivalry was their 108–107 victory in 1993. It took three **overtimes** before the Tigers won. Illini fans have a different idea. They might vote for a game that took place five years earlier. When Illinois and Missouri met that season, both were ranked in the Top 10.

The Illini celebrate with the Braggin' Rights trophy after the team's victory over Missouri in December of 2003.

The Illini were undefeated when the game began. After 14 minutes, Missouri was ahead by 18 points. The Tigers were teasing the Illinois players. Nick Anderson looked his opponents in the eye and said, "This game is far from over."

Anderson was right. Kenny Battle, Marcus Liberty, and Steve Bardo scored 11 points in a row to cut the lead to seven at halftime. In the second half, the Illini came out flying. They ran up and down the court, causing **turnovers** with their **full-court press** and scoring on fast breaks. Battle scored 19 points in the last 20 minutes, including the winning free throws with time running out. Illinois ran off the court with an unforgettable 87–84 victory.

One Great Day

Picking the greatest day in Illinois basketball history is almost impossible. There are simply too many to choose from. There was the victory over superstar George Mikan and top-ranked DePaul in 1945. There was Dave Downey's 53-point game against Indiana in 1963. And there was the last-second shot by Derek Harper in 1983. That basket started a streak of eight trips to the NCAA Tournament.

For pure excitement and drama, however, nothing beats the season's last game against Minnesota in 2002. Illinois entered the year hoping to repeat as conference champs. After a slow start in the Big Ten, the Illini caught fire and won seven games in a row. They needed one more victory to claim a share of the conference title.

The game was played on Minnesota's home court. The Golden Gophers built a big lead in the second half. With three minutes left, the Illini trailed by nine points. They refused to give up.

Cory Bradford hit a long 3-pointer, and Robert Archibald made two free throws to make the score 66–62. Brian Cook blocked a Minnesota shot and the ball went to Archibald, who was fouled again. This time he missed his free throws. There were only 31 seconds left. "We had no

Luther Head runs to congratulate Frank Williams, who jumps for joy after his game-winning shot against Minnesota.

chance to win that game at that point," coach Bill Self remembers.

Frank Williams thought differently. He tried to rip the ball from the hands of Minnesota's Kerwin Fleming. Somehow he did so without committing a foul. Bradford scooped up the ball and made another 3-pointer to bring Illinois within one point. Illinois then forced Minnesota to throw a pass out of bounds with six seconds left. Self called timeout. The confident Williams looked at his teammates and said, "Give me the ball."

Williams got the ball on the right side. Travarus Bennett, the Big Ten Defensive Player of the Year, stood between him and the basket. Williams broke for the hoop and rose into the air. Bennett was right there with him. Instead of shooting, Williams hung in the air and pulled the ball back. Bennett flew past him, and Williams made a soft bank shot before the buzzer sounded for an amazing 67–66 win. For the first time in 50 years, the Illini could say they were back-to-back Big Ten champs.

It Really Happened

When a talented team opens up a big lead in the second half of an NCAA Tournament game, many fans watching on TV turn the channel. Those who gave up on Illinois during the fourth round of the 2005 NCAA Tournament are still kicking themselves. After a close and exciting first half, the Illini could not hit a shot against the Arizona Wildcats. With four minutes left in the contest, the score was 75–60.

Illinois had not trailed an opponent by more than nine points all year. But coach Bruce Weber told his players not to give up. The Wildcats were exhausted, he said. They had nothing left. Weber urged his team to dig in on defense. If the Illini made their shots on offense, they still had a chance.

The Illinois defense turned up the heat. The team allowed only five points the rest of the way. On offense, the Illini began hitting 3-pointers and layups. Deron Williams and Luther Head took charge and connected on one shot after another.

With less than a minute left, Arizona's lead was down to 80–77. The Wildcats made a bad pass and lost the ball. Williams rose off the floor and hit a 3-pointer to tie the game. In overtime, Williams and Head

Deron Williams rises for a 3-point shot in the final minutes of the Illini's win over Arizona.

stayed in control. Illinois scored 10 points and then prepared for a final charge by the Wildcats.

With the score 90–89, Arizona had one last chance. Hassan Adams took a long shot at the buzzer. The Illini and their fans held their breath as the ball sailed through the air—and jumped for joy when it missed the rim. Illinois had earned a trip to the Final Four with one of the most amazing wins in NCAA Tournament history.

Team Spirit

Orange and navy blue are the school colors at Illinois. But when Illini fans get together, only one of the two is needed to show team spirit. Orange says it all at the school. In fact, for many years, Illinois held a special "Paint the Hall Orange" game. Everyone wore orange. It was quite a sight! Today, almost everyone wears orange to every home game.

Illinois basketball fans are loud, proud, and loyal. Students are encouraged to sit in sections close to the court known as the "Orange Krush." From there, they lead the crowd in cheers and songs. The school fight song is called "Oskee Wow Wow." It was written back in 1911. The school band plays it during warm-ups and timeouts.

The team's most important tradition is welcoming the state's best players. Where would the Illini be without them! Luckily, it is also a tradition for high school stars around the state to dream about playing for Illinois. Marcus Liberty said it best when he explained, "Following the guys from Chicago who were Illini before me was really special."

Students at Illinois love to show their team spirit as part of the "Orange Krush." When they get excited, they help the players raise their energy level on the court.

Timeline

The basketball season is played from October through March. That means each season takes place at the end of one year and the beginning of the next. In this timeline, the accomplishments of the team are shown by season.

1905–06
Illinois wins its first official game by a score of 71–4.

1951–52
Illinois reaches the Final Four.

1964–65
Skip Thoren sets a team rebounding record.

1941–42
All five starters are honored as All-Americans.

1962–63
Dave Downey scores 53 points in a game.

1972–73
Nick Weatherspoon is named an All-American.

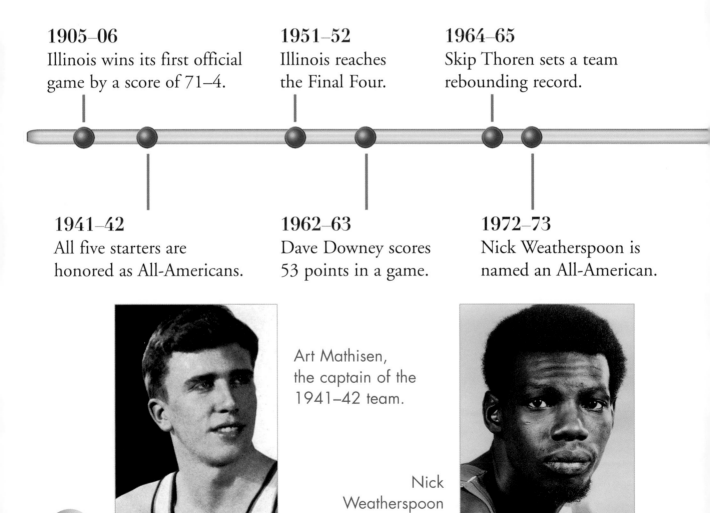

Art Mathisen, the captain of the 1941–42 team.

Nick Weatherspoon

A program from the Illini's game against Michigan State.

Chester Frazier gets ready to play defense.

1978–79
The Illini beat Magic Johnson and top-ranked Michigan State.

1993–94
Deon Thomas is named team MVP for the third year in a row.

2008–09
Chester Frazier is named to the Big Ten **All-Defensive Team**.

1988–89
Illinois returns to the Final Four.

2003–04
Bruce Weber becomes the team's coach.

2004 05
The Illini reach the NCAA championship game.

Bruce Weber and Roger Powell celebrate during the 2004–05 season.

Fun Facts

SPEED READER

Johnny Kerr was a great passing center. Why was that? The answer is soccer. The sport was Kerr's first love as a teenager, and he was great at "reading" the field and finding open teammates. When he sprouted to nearly seven feet, he was too tall for soccer and switched to basketball.

LIVING LARGE

One of the most amazing performances in school history came in a loss. In 1972, 6′ 6″ Nick Conner outplayed 7′ 0″ Bill Walton of UCLA, but the Illini lost 71–64. Walton was named Player of the Year, and the Bruins went 30–0 to win the national championship.

LONG SHOT

The greatest basket in school history may belong to Bob Starnes. In a 1963 game against Northwestern, Starnes broke a 76–76 tie at the buzzer with a shot from the free throw line—his own free throw line! The ball traveled nearly 60 feet in the air before swishing through the net.

Lou Boudreau

PLAY BALL!

The star forward for the Illini in 1936–37 was Lou Boudreau. He captained the team a year later. Boudreau went on to become a great baseball player who made it to the *Hall of Fame*.

HEAD GAMES

The leading scorer on the 2004–05 team was not Deron Williams. It was Luther Head. That season, Head set a school record for 3-pointers with 116.

SHOOTING STAR

From 1998 to 2001, Cory Bradford made at least one 3-pointer in 88 games in a row. The first came in his first game as a freshman. The last came when Bradford was a junior. His streak set an NCAA record.

FAREWELL PERFORMANCE

In his last game before enlisting in the army in 1943, Andy Phillip took 54 shots against the University of Chicago. That total set a school record.

For the Record

The great Illinois teams, coaches, and players have left their marks on the record books. These are the "best of the best" ...

FIGHTING ILLINI AWARD WINNERS

PLAYER OF THE YEAR		BIG TEN DEFENSIVE PLAYER OF THE YEAR	
Ray Woods	1916–17	Bruce Douglas	1984–85
Chuck Carney	1921–22	Bruce Douglas	1985–86
Andy Phillip	1942–43	Steve Bardo	1988–89
Dee Brown	2004–05	Dee Brown	2004–05

BIG TEN PLAYER OF THE YEAR		BIG TEN FRESHMAN OF THE YEAR	
Kenny Battle*	1983–84	Cory Bradford	1998–99
Frank Williams	2000–01	Brian Cook*	1999–00
Brian Cook	2002–03		
Dee Brown	2004–05		

Shared this honor with another player.

A photo signed by Bruce Weber shows him with the team's many championship trophies.

ILLINOIS BASKETBALL HEAD COACH BRUCE WEBER

FIGHTING ILLINI ACHIEVEMENTS

ACHIEVEMENT	YEAR
Big Ten Champions	1914–15
NCAA Champions*	1914–15
Big Ten Champions**	1916–17
Big Ten Champions**	1923–24
Big Ten Champions**	1934–35
Big Ten Champions**	1936–37
Big Ten Champions	1941–42
Big Ten Champions	1942–43
Big Ten Champions	1948–49
Big Ten Champions	1950–51
Big Ten Champions	1951–52
Big Ten Champions**	1962–63
Big Ten Champions**	1983–84
Big Ten Champions**	1997–98
Big Ten Champions**	2000–01
Big Ten Champions**	2001–02
Big Ten Tournament Champions	2002–03
Big Ten Champions	2003–04
Big Ten Champions	2004–05
Big Ten Tournament Champions	2004–05
NCAA Finalists	2004–05

* Honor awarded later by the Helms Foundation.
** Shared this honor with another school.

LEFT: Cory Bradford, the 1998–99 Big Ten Freshman of the Year.
TOP RIGHT: 2004–05 Big Ten Player of the Year Dee Brown was front-page news during the 2005 NCAA Tournament.
BOTTOM RIGHT: This old button shows Chief Illiniwek, the team's former mascot.

The Big Ten

The University of Illinois is a member of the Big Ten Conference, the oldest college sports conference in America. Over the years, the Big Ten actually expanded to 11 teams. These are the Fighting Illinis' neighbors …

THE BIG TEN

1 University of Illinois Fighting Illini
Urbana-Champaign, Illinois

2 Indiana University Hoosiers
Bloomington, Indiana

3 University of Iowa Hawkeyes
Iowa City, Iowa

4 University of Michigan Wolverines
Ann Arbor, Michigan

5 Michigan State University Spartans
East Lansing, Michigan

6 University of Minnesota Golden Gophers
Minneapolis and Saint Paul, Minnesota

7 Northwestern University Wildcats
Evanston, Illinois

8 Ohio State University Buckeyes
Columbus, Ohio

9 Pennsylvania State University Nittany Lions*
University Park, Pennsylvania

10 Purdue University Boilermakers
West Lafayette, Indiana

11 University of Wisconsin Badgers
Madison, Wisconsin

* Penn State joined the Big Ten in 1993.

The College Game

Coll>ollege basketball may look like the same game you see professional teams play, but there are some important differences. The first is that college teams play half as many games as the pros do. That's because the players have to attend classes, write papers, and study for exams! Below are several other differences between college and pro basketball.

CLASS NOTES

Most college players are younger than pro players. They are student-athletes who have graduated from high school and now play on their school's varsity team, which is the highest level of competition. Most are between the ages of 18 and 22.

College players are allowed to compete for four seasons. Each year is given a different name or "class"—freshman (first year), sophomore (second year), junior (third year), and senior (fourth year). Sometimes highly skilled players leave college before graduation to play in the pros.

RULE BOOK

There are several differences between the rules in college basketball and the NBA. Here are the most important ones: 1) In college, games last 40 minutes. Teams play two 20-minute halves. In the pros, teams play 48-minute games, divided into four 12-minute quarters. 2) In college, players are disqualified after five personal fouls. In the pros, that number is six. 3) In college, the 3-point line is 20′ 9″ from the basket. In the pros, the line is three feet farther away.

WHO'S NUMBER 1?

How is the national championship of basketball decided? At the end of each season, the top teams are invited to play in the NCAA Tournament. The teams are divided into four groups, and the winner of each group advances to the Final Four. The Final Four consists of two semifinal games. The winners then play for the championship of college basketball.

CONFERENCE CALL

College basketball teams are members of athletic conferences. Each conference represents a different part of the country. For example, the Atlantic Coast Conference is made up of teams from up and down the East Coast. Teams that belong to the same conference usually play each other twice—once on each school's home court. Teams also play games outside their conference. Wins and losses in these games do not count in the conference standings. However, they are very important to a team's national ranking.

TOURNAMENT TIME

At the end of the year, most conferences hold a championship tournament. A team can have a poor record and still be invited to play in the NCAA Tournament if it wins the conference tournament. For many schools, this is an exciting "second chance." In most cases, the regular-season winner and conference tournament winner are given spots in the national tournament. The rest of the tournament "bids" are given to the best remaining teams.

Glossary

BASKETBALL WORDS TO KNOW

3-POINTERS—Baskets made from behind the 3-point line.

ALL-AMERICAN—A college player voted as the best at his position.

ALL-AROUND—Good at all parts of the game.

ALL-BIG TEN—An honor given each year to the conference's best players at each position.

ALL-DEFENSIVE TEAM—An honor given at the end of each season to a conference's best defensive players at each position.

ALL-FINAL FOUR—An honor given to the best players among the last four teams remaining in the NCAA Tournament.

ASSISTS—Passes that lead to successful shots.

BIG TEN CONFERENCE—A conference for colleges located in Illinois, Indiana, Iowa, Michigan, Minnesota, Ohio, Pennsylvania, and Wisconsin. The Big Ten was formed in 1896.

BIG TEN TOURNAMENT—The competition that decides the champion of the conference.

DOUBLE-TEAM—Guard an opponent with two defenders.

DRAFT PICK—A college player selected or "drafted" by NBA teams each summer.

DRIVING—Making a strong move to the basket.

FAST BREAK—A style of offense in which the team with the ball rushes down the court to take a shot.

FINAL FOUR—The term for the last four teams remaining in the NCAA Tournament.

FULL-COURT PRESS—A defensive game plan in which a team pressures the opponent for the entire length of the court.

LINEUP—The list of players who are playing in a game.

LOOSE BALLS—Balls that are not controlled by either team.

MOST OUTSTANDING PLAYER (MOP)—The award given each year to the best player in the Big Ten Tournament. It is also awarded to the best player in the NCAA Tournament.

MOST VALUABLE PLAYER (MVP)—The award given each year to a conference's best player.

NATIONAL BASKETBALL ASSOCIATION (NBA)—The league that has been operating since 1946–47.

NATIONAL COLLEGIATE ATHLETIC ASSOCIATION (NCAA)—The organization that oversees the majority of college sports.

NCAA TOURNAMENT—The competition that determines the champion of college basketball.

OVERTIMES—The extra periods played when a game is tied after 40 minutes and then again after each extra period that ends in a tie.

PLAYMAKER—Someone who helps his teammates score by passing the ball.

POSTSEASON—A term for games played after the regular season.

RECRUIT—Offer an athletic scholarship to a prospective student. College teams compete for the best high school players every year.

ROSTER—The list of players on a team.

TEAM BASKETBALL—A style of play that involves everyone on the court instead of just one or two stars.

TURNOVERS—Plays in which the team on offense loses possession of the ball.

OTHER WORDS TO KNOW

ARCHITECT—Someone who designs buildings and other structures.

ATHLETIC DIRECTOR—The person in charge of a college's sports programs.

CAMPUS—The grounds and buildings of a college.

CENTURY—A period of 100 years.

COMEBACK—The process of catching up from behind, or making up a large deficit.

DECADES—Periods of 10 years; also specific periods, such as the 1950s.

HALL OF FAME—The museum in Cooperstown, New York, where baseball's greatest players are honored.

INHERITED—Came into a situation left by others.

LOGO—A symbol or design that represents a company or team.

MASCOT—An animal or person believed to bring a group good luck.

OLYMPICS—An international sports competition held every four years.

OVATION—A long, loud cheer.

RIVAL—Extremely emotional competitor.

ROSE BOWL—The annual football bowl game played in Pasadena, California. The Tournament of Roses Parade takes place before the game.

SATIN—A smooth, shiny fabric.

SUBURBS—Communities surrounding a major city.

SYMBOLS—Things that represent a thought or idea.

SYNTHETIC—Made in a laboratory, not in nature.

TRADITION—A belief or custom that is handed down from generation to generation.

Places to Go
ON THE ROAD

UNIVERSITY OF ILLINOIS FIGHTING ILLINI
1800 South 1st Street
Champaign, Illinois 61820
(217) 333-3400

NAISMITH MEMORIAL BASKETBALL HALL OF FAME
1000 West Columbus Avenue
Springfield, Massachusetts 01105
(877) 4HOOPLA

ON THE WEB

THE UNIVERSITY OF ILLINOIS FIGHTING ILLINI   www.fightingillini.com
• *Learn more about the Fighting Illini*

BIG TEN CONFERENCE   bigten.cstv.com
• *Learn more about the Big Ten teams*

THE BASKETBALL HALL OF FAME   www.hoophall.com
• *Learn more about history's greatest players*

ON THE BOOKSHELF

To learn more about the sport of basketball, look for these books at your library or bookstore:

• Kaufman, Gabriel. *Basketball in the Big Ten Conference.* New York, New York: Rosen Central, 2008.

• Labrecque, Ellen. *Basketball.* Ann Arbor, Michigan: Cherry Lake Publishing, 2009.

• Stewart, Mark and Kennedy, Mike. *Swish: the Quest for Basketball's Perfect Shot.* Minneapolis, Minnesota: Millbrook Press, 2009.

Index

About the Author

MARK STEWART has written more than 30 books on basketball players and teams, and over 100 sports books for kids. He has also interviewed dozens of athletes, politicians, and celebrities. Although Mark grew up in New York City, this is his second book on the University of Illinois. His first, *Rush to Judgment*, was about Illini football star Simeon Rice. Mark comes from a family of writers. His grandfather was Sunday Editor of *The New York Times* and his mother was Articles Editor for *Ladies' Home Journal* and *McCall's*. Mark became interested in sports during lazy summer days spent at the Connecticut home of his father's godfather, sportswriter John R. Tunis. Mark is a graduate of Duke University, with a degree in History. He lives with his wife Sarah, and daughters Mariah and Rachel, overlooking Sandy Hook, New Jersey.

MATT ZEYSING is the resident historian at the Basketball Hall of Fame in Springfield, Massachusetts. His research interests include the origins of the game of basketball, the development of professional basketball in the first half of the 20th century, and the culture and meaning of basketball in American society.